**THIS YUMMI BUDDI
COLORING BOOK
BELONGS TO**

_____

COPYRIGHTS 2020 YUMMI BUDDI BOOKS
ILLUSTRATED BY BENITO DELGADO

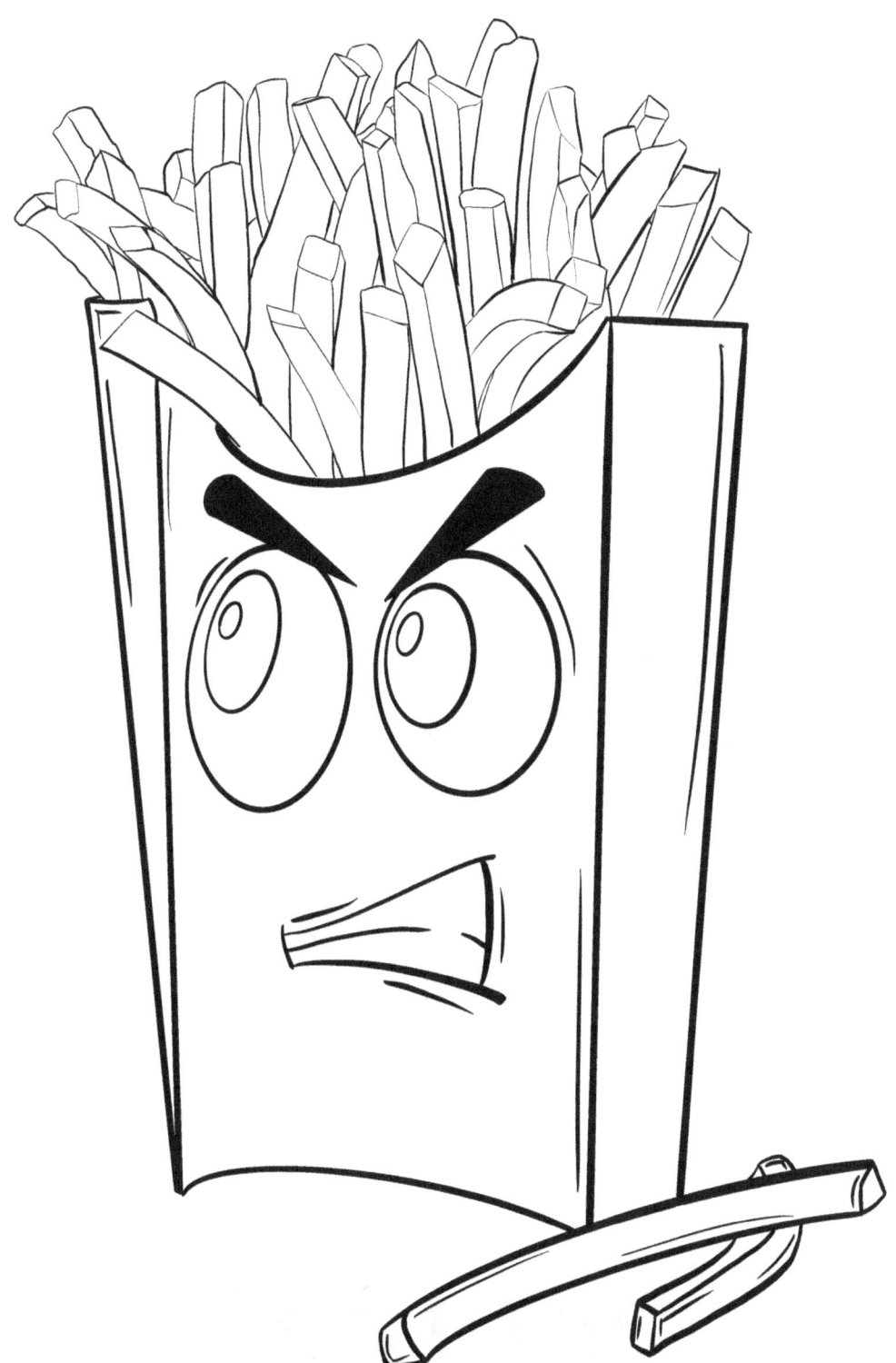

MR.FRIES

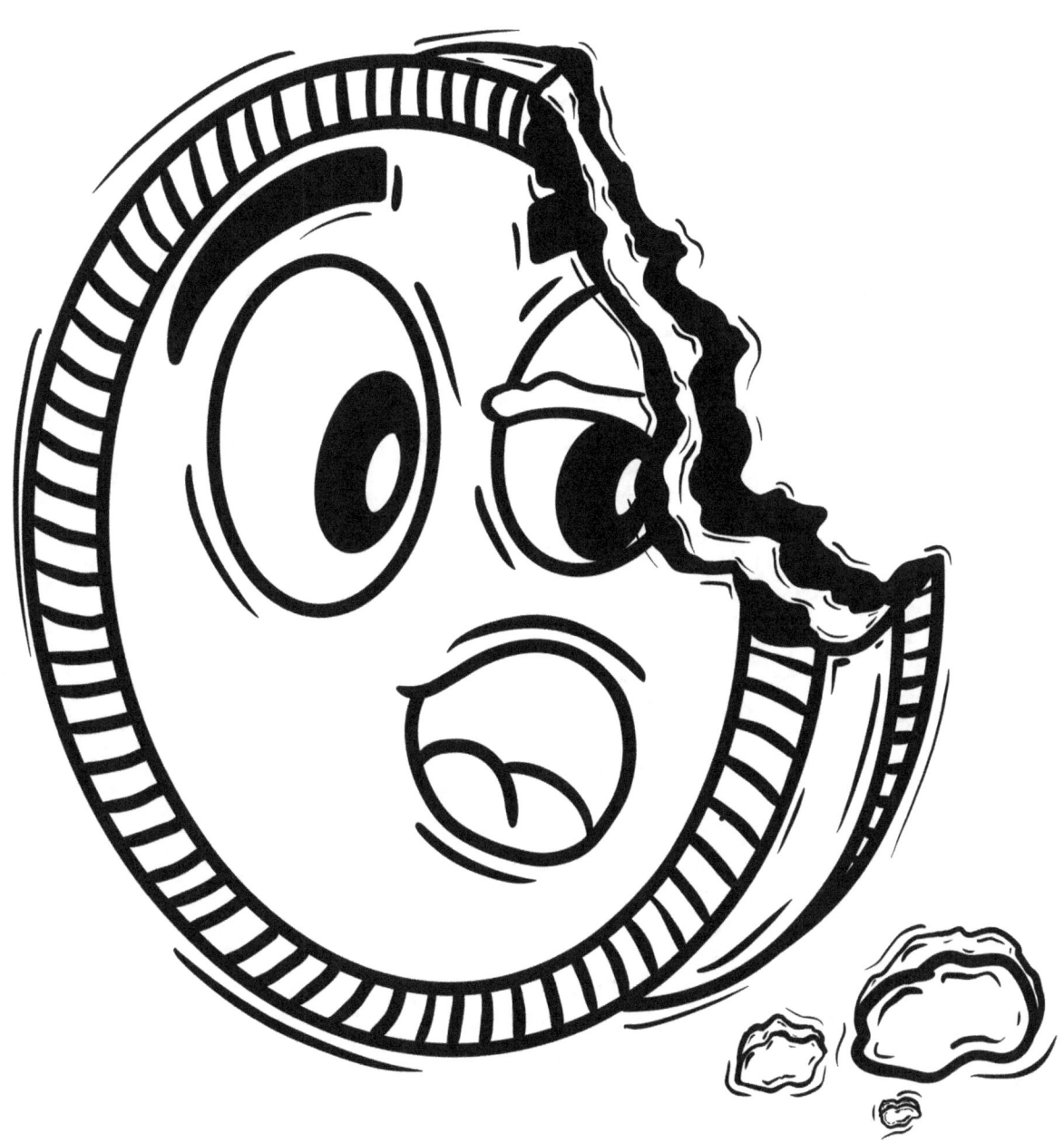

COOKIE

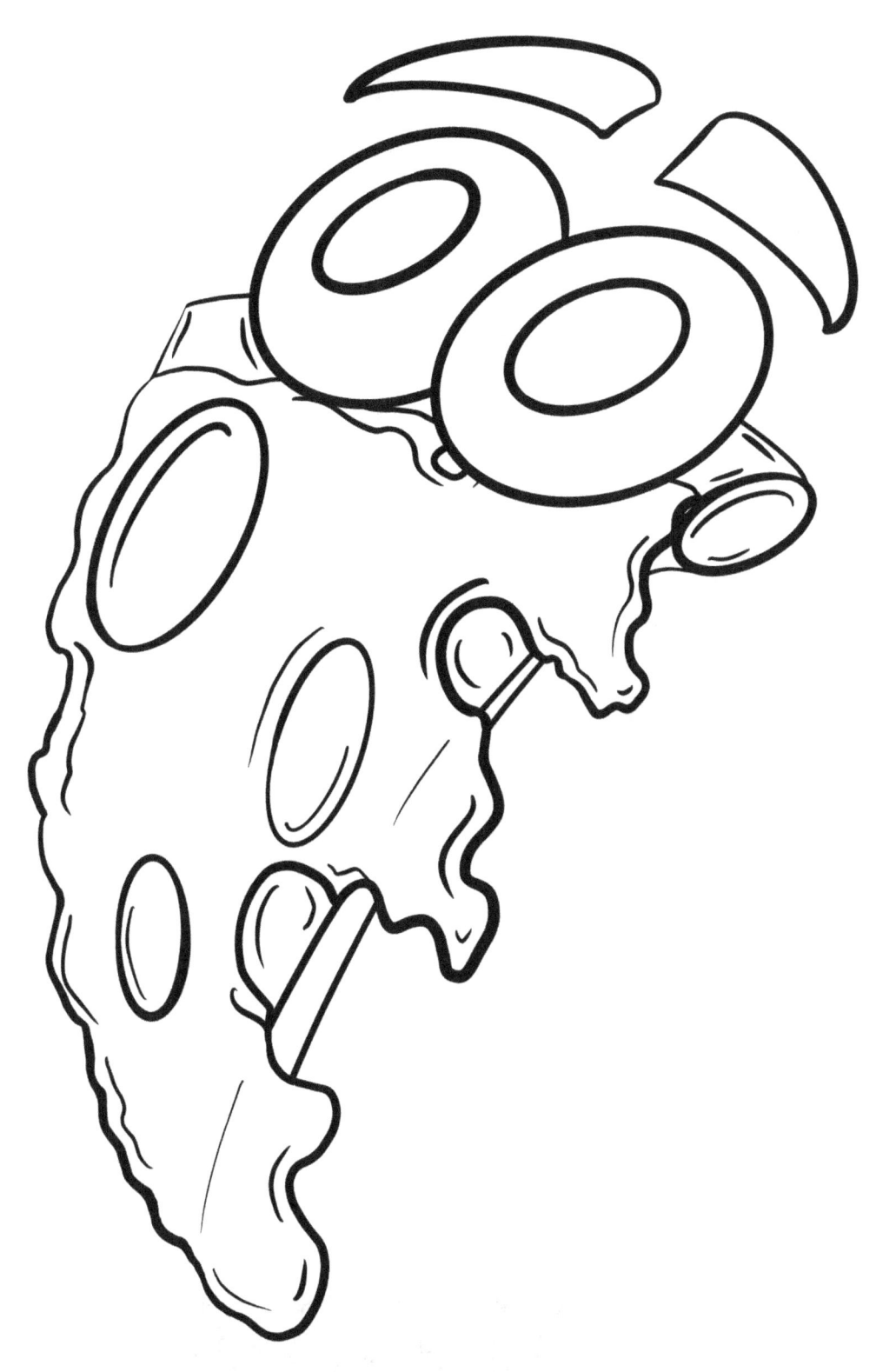

PIZZABOY

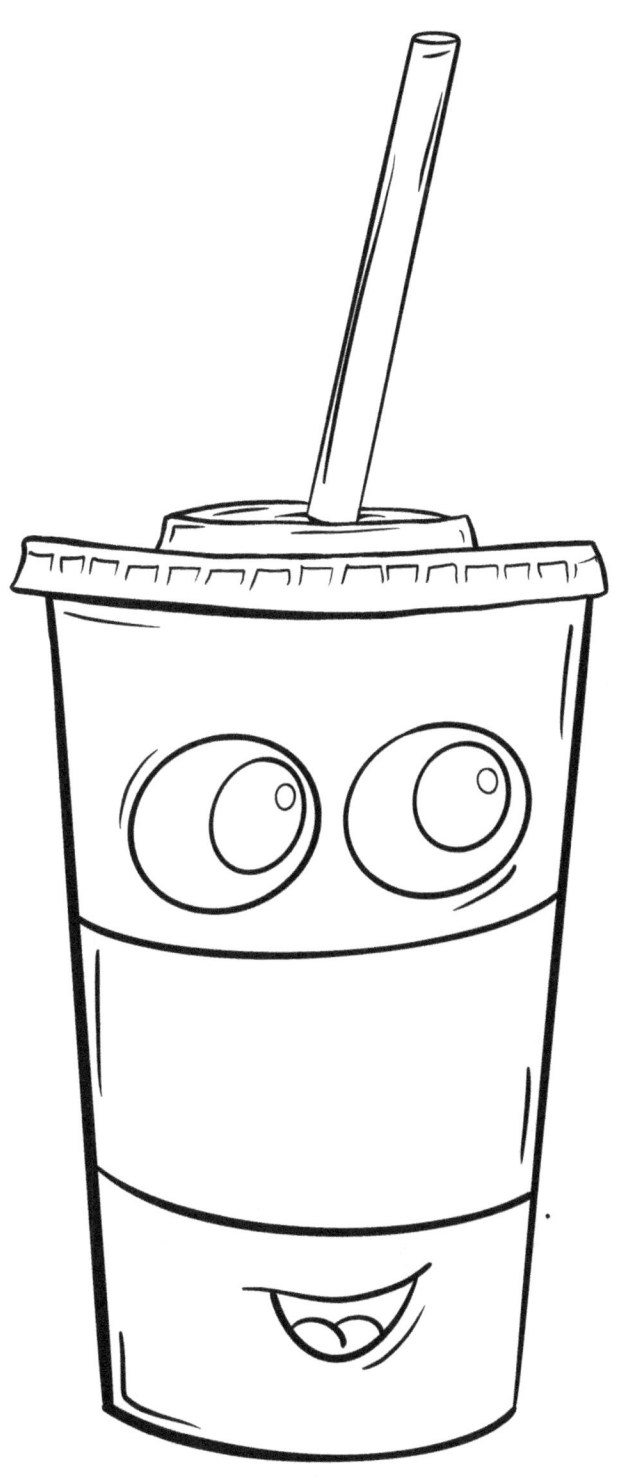

MR. CUPPI

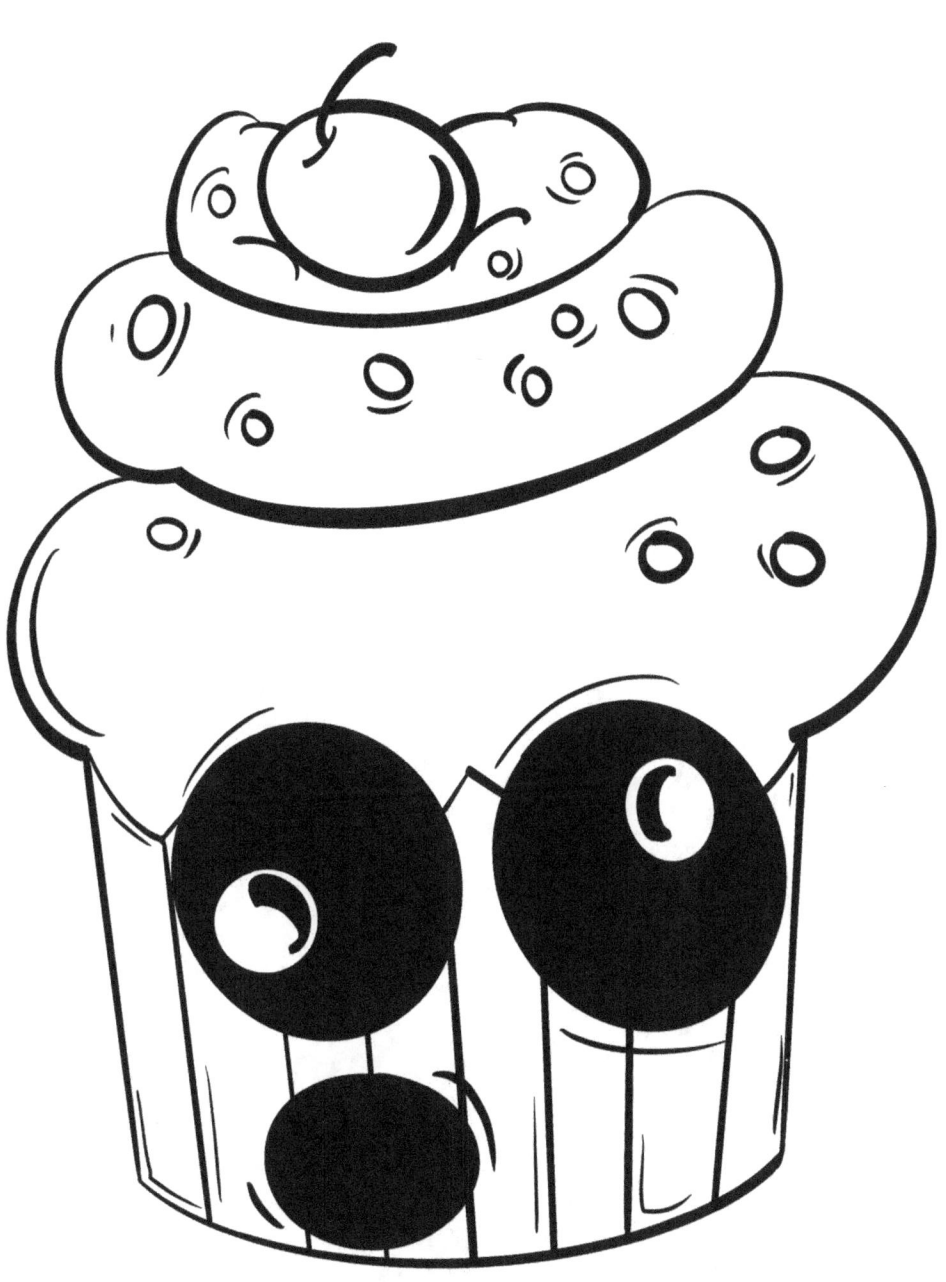

CRAZY CAKE

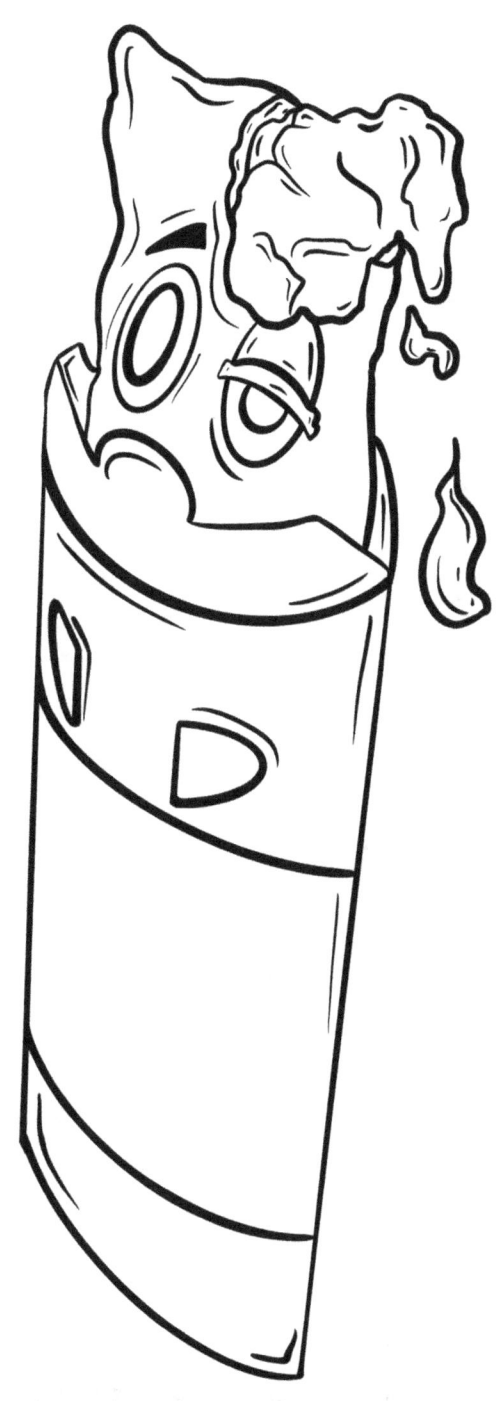

BABY PIE

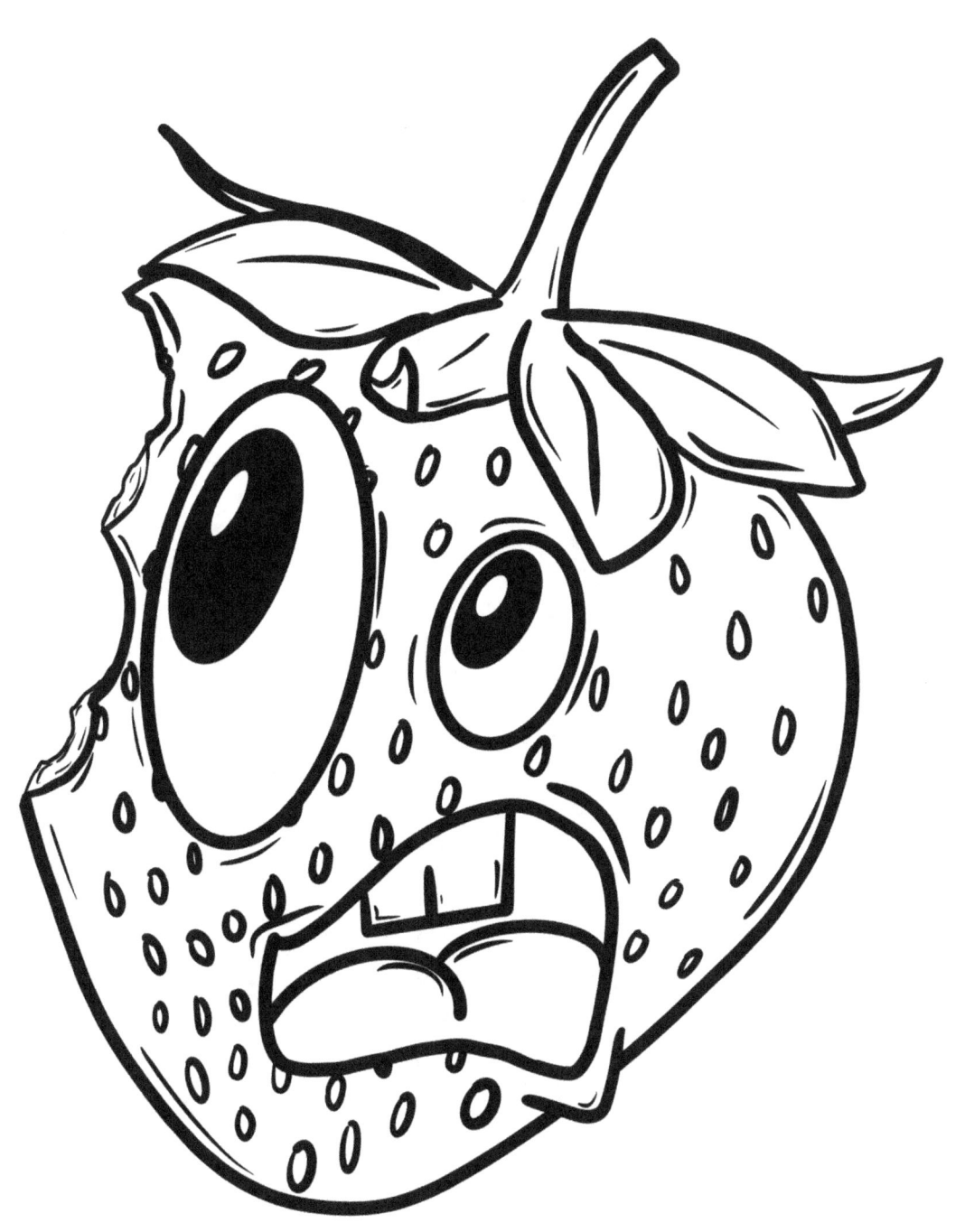

STRAWBURRY

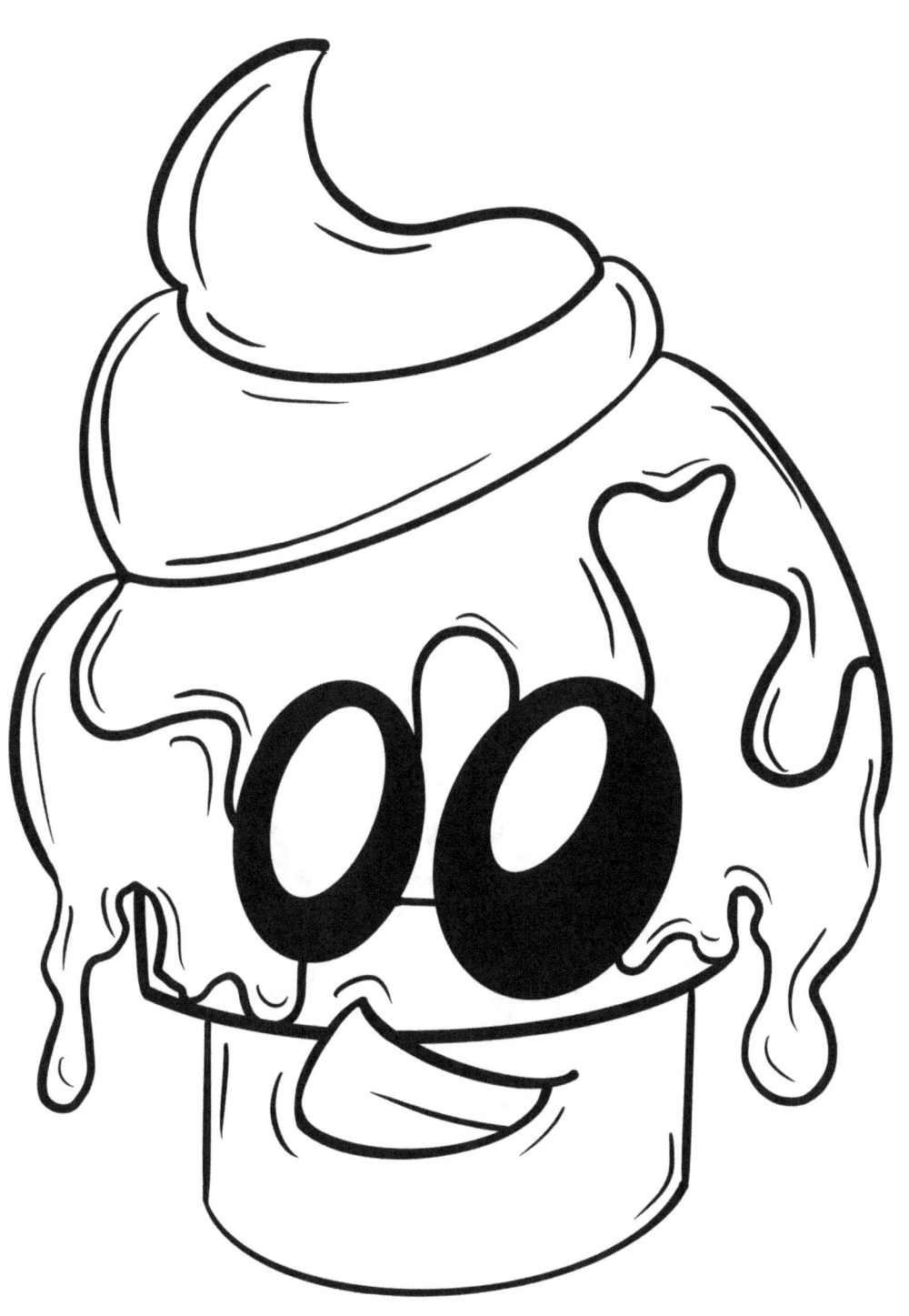

ICECONE

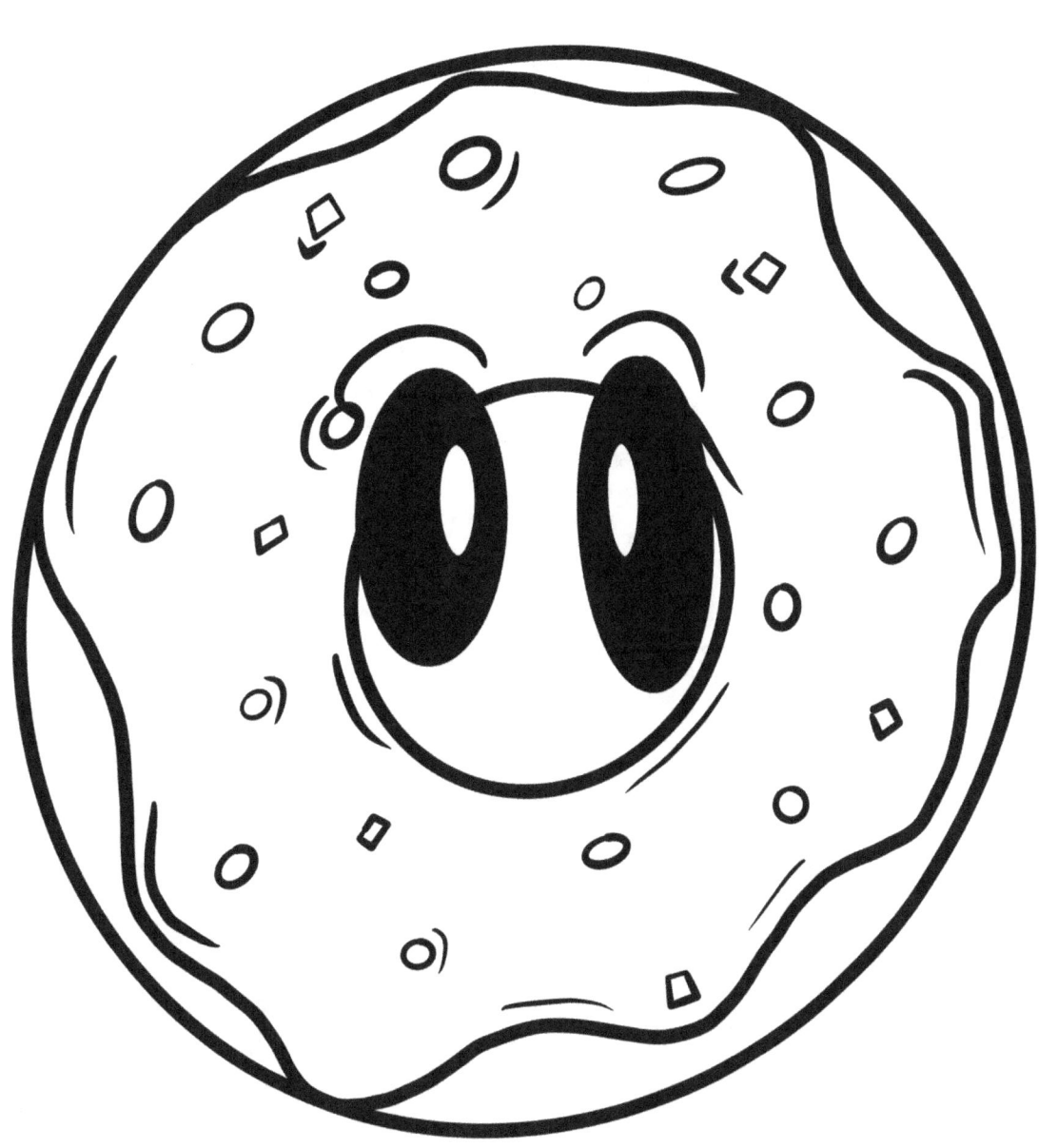

BABY DOUGHNUT

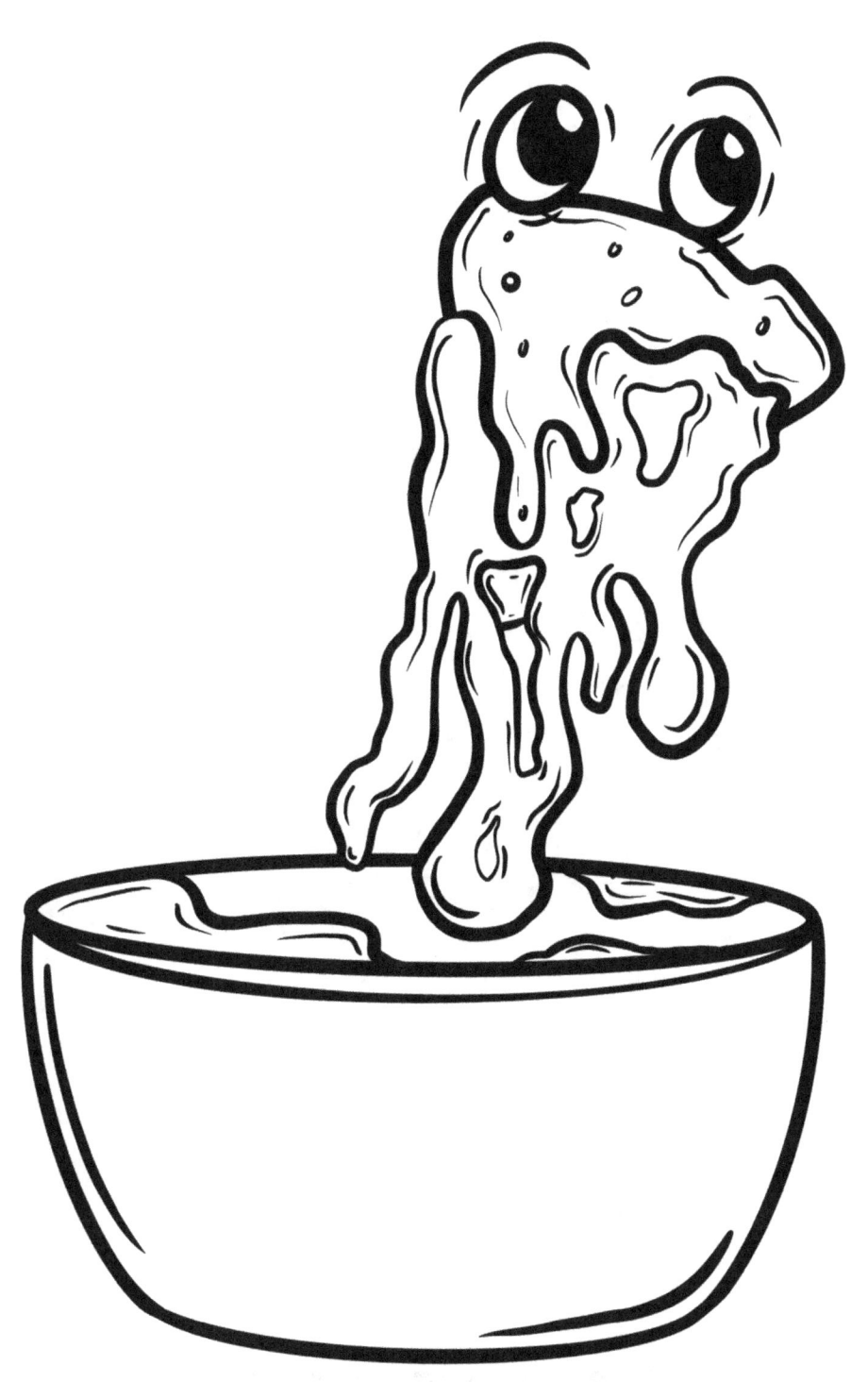

EL NACHO

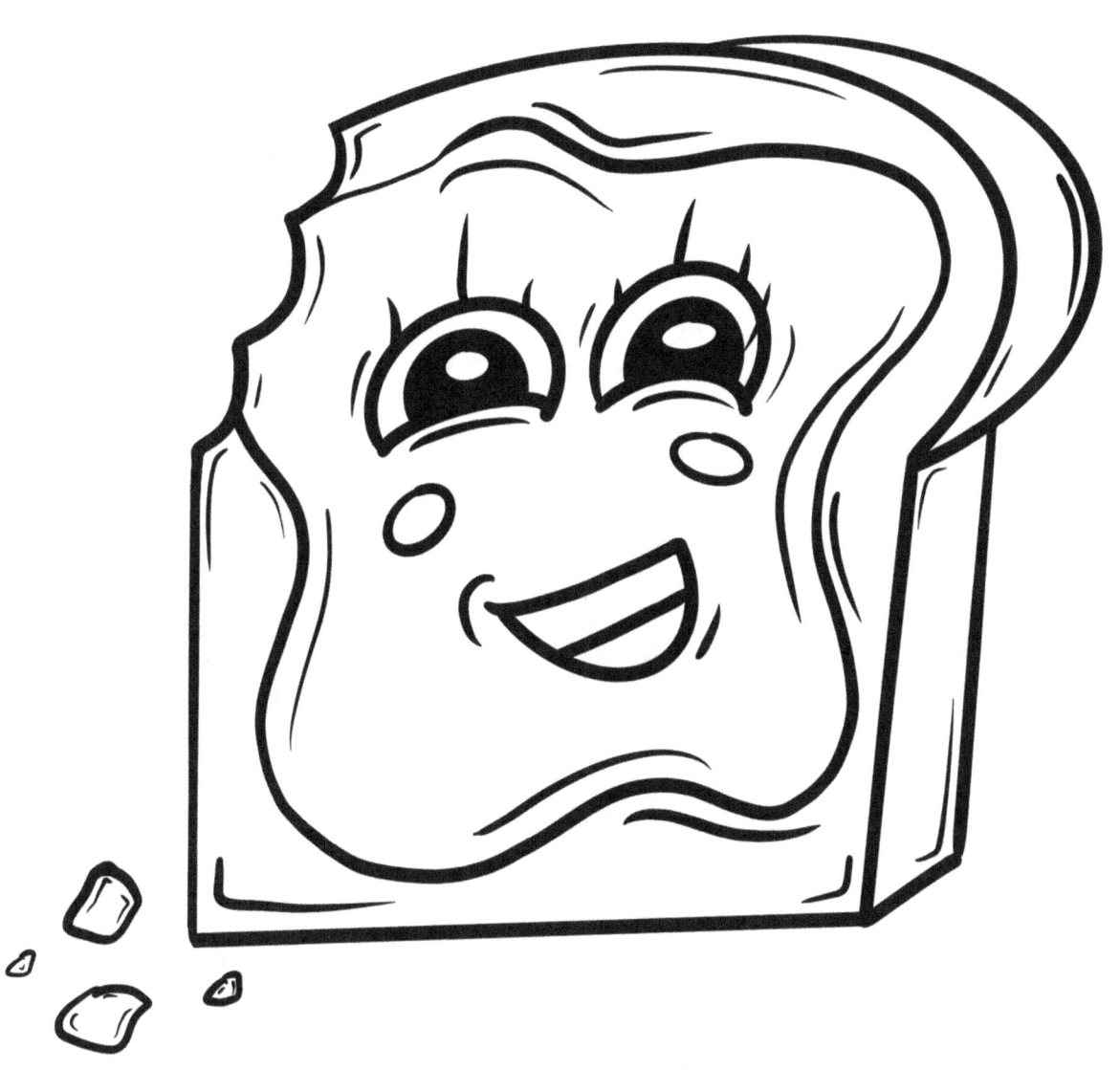

FRENCH TOAST N' JELLY

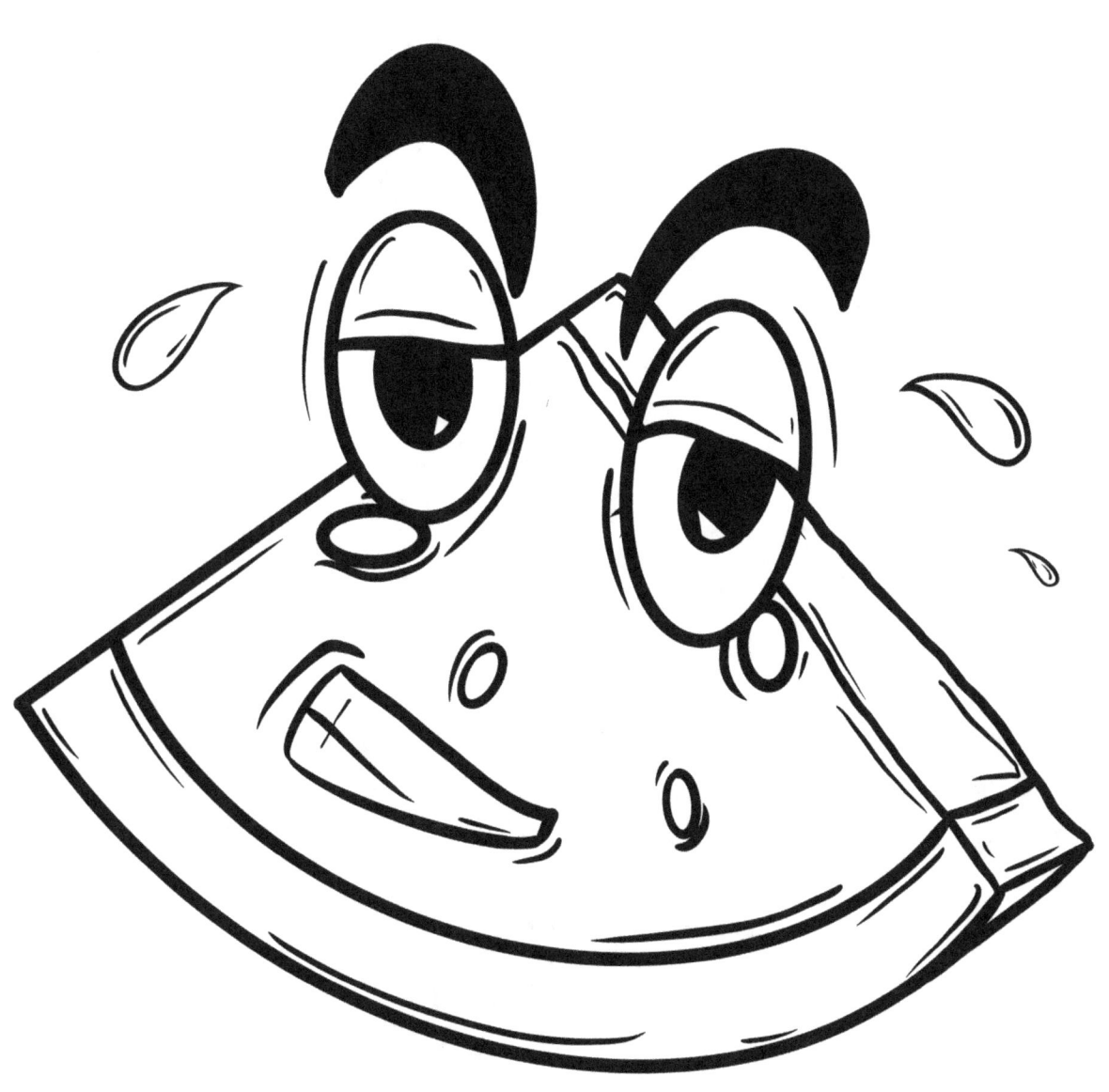

EL WATERMAELON

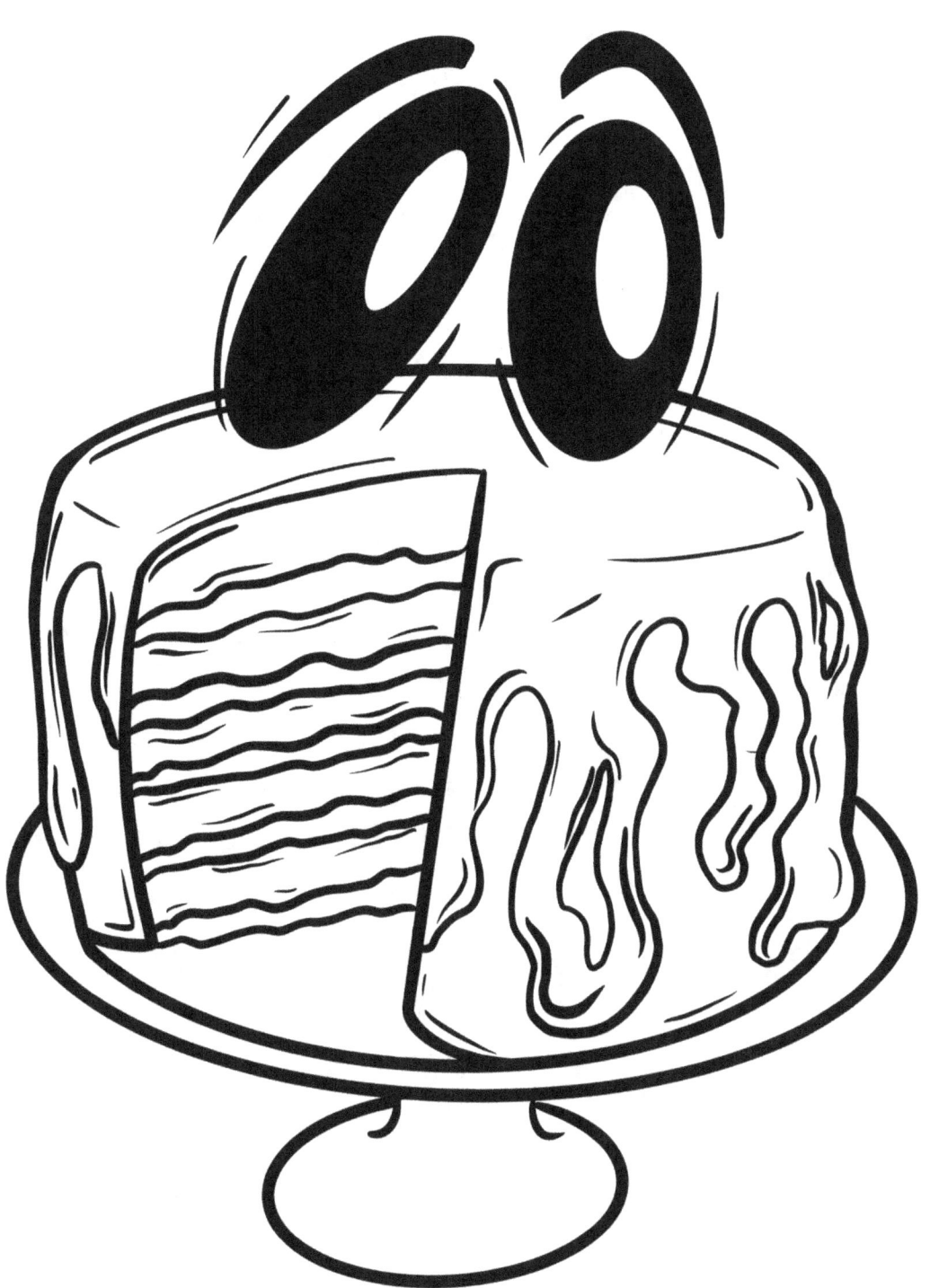

BIG CAKES

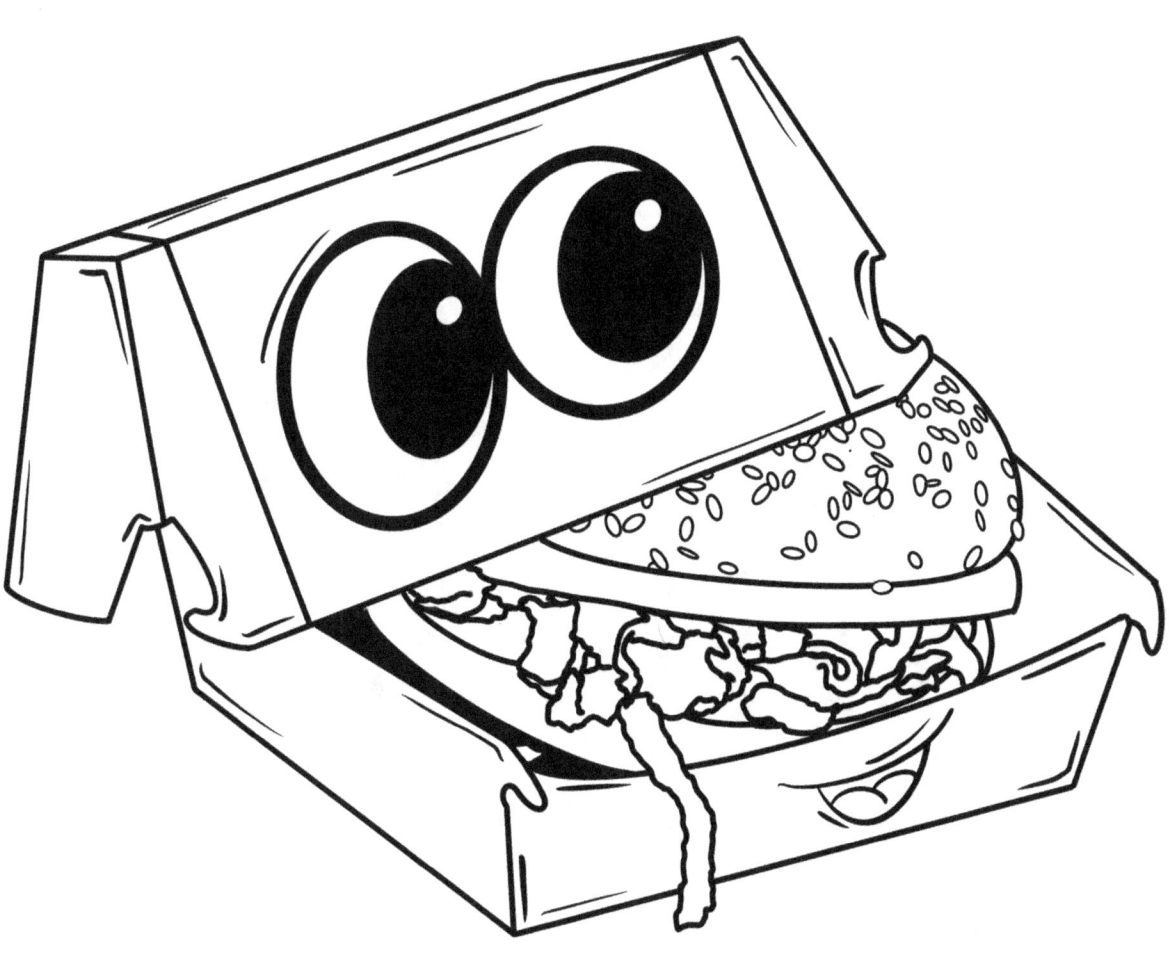

EL BURGER

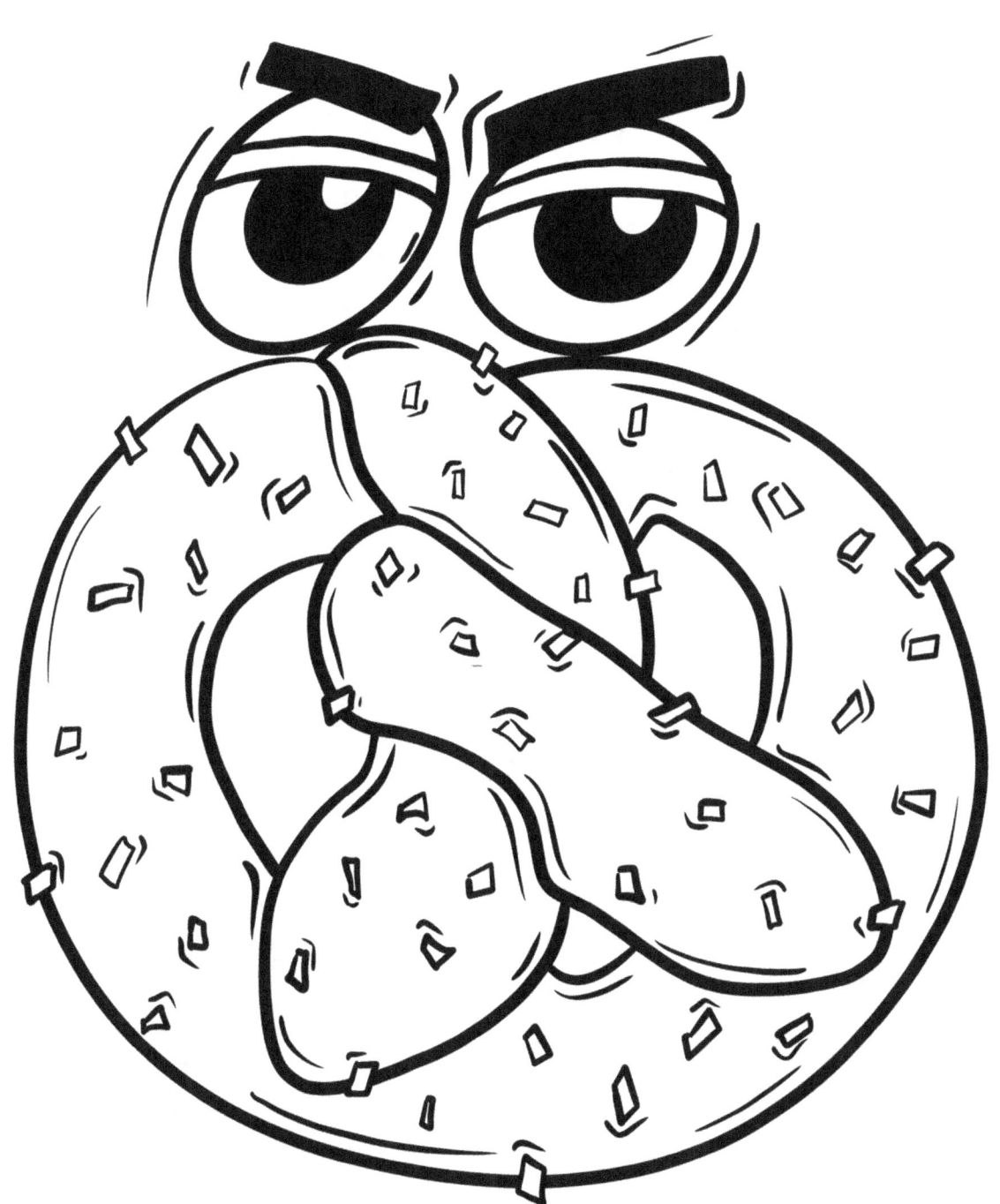

ANGRY PRETZEL BOY

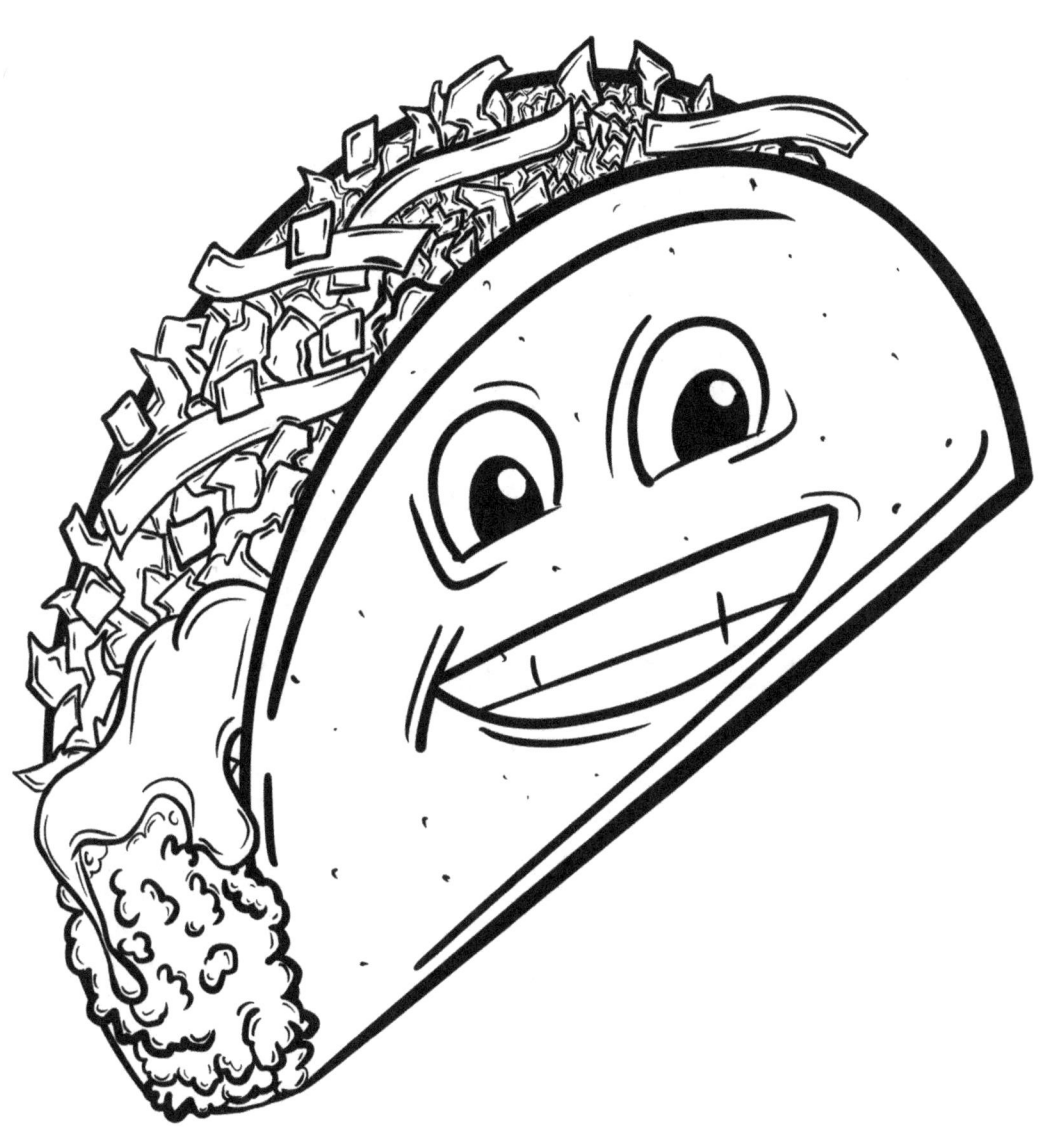

THE TACO

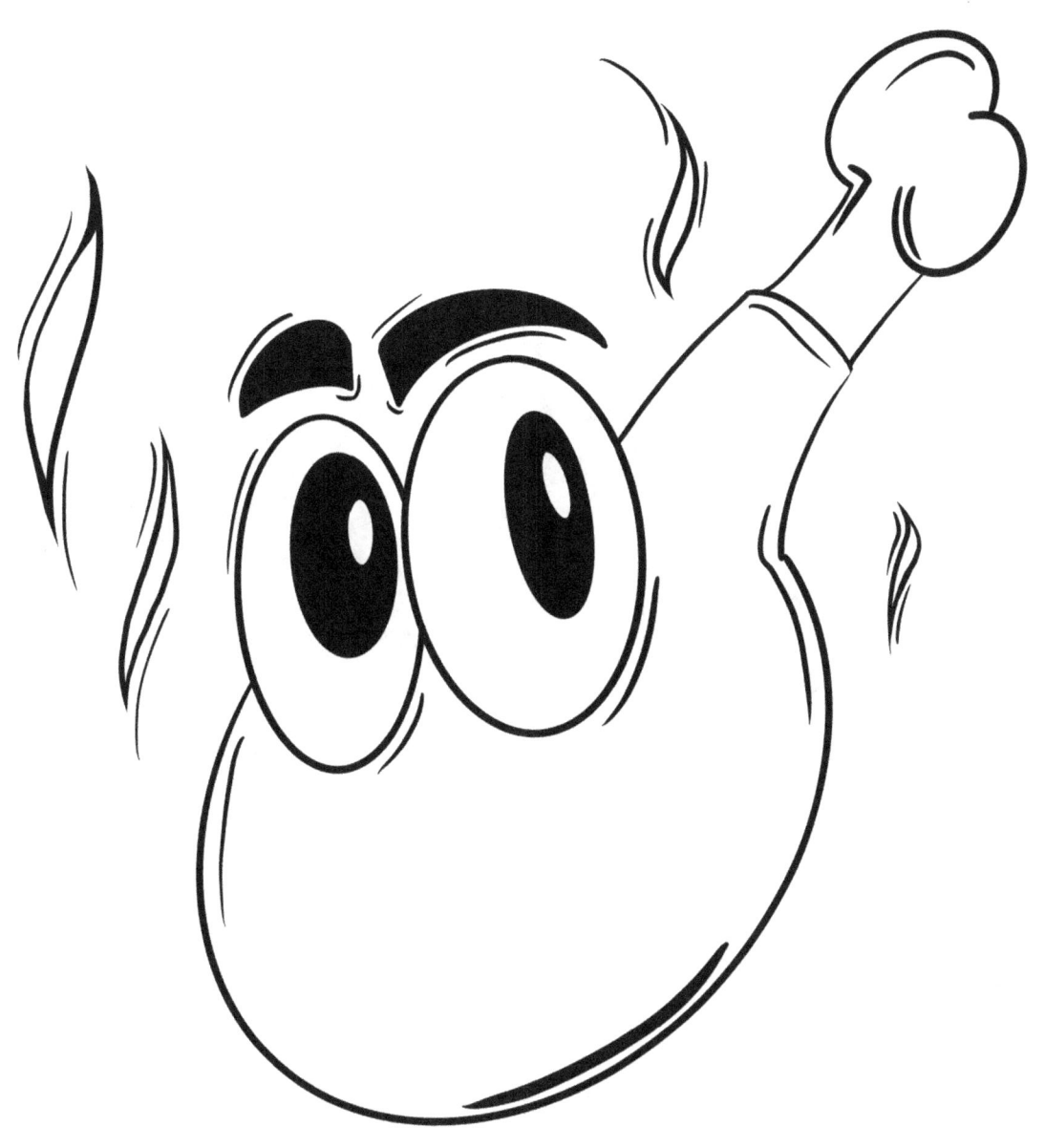

CHICKEN LEG

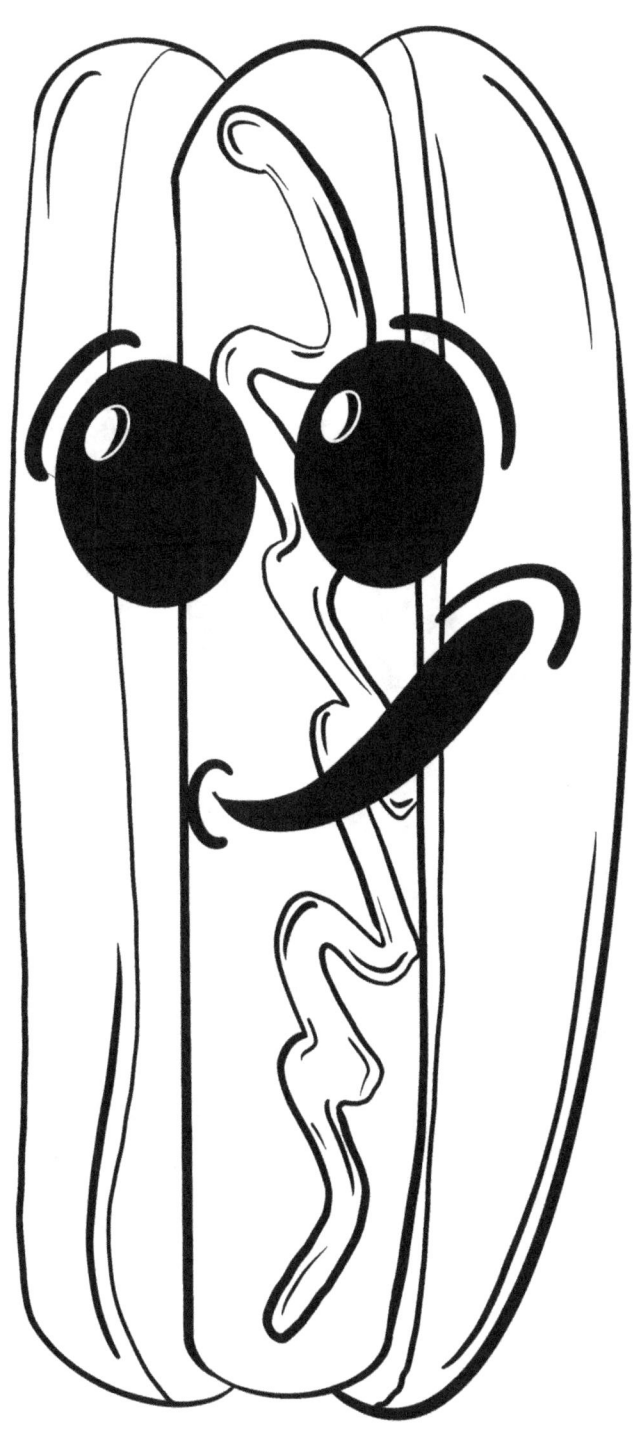

THE HOTDAWG

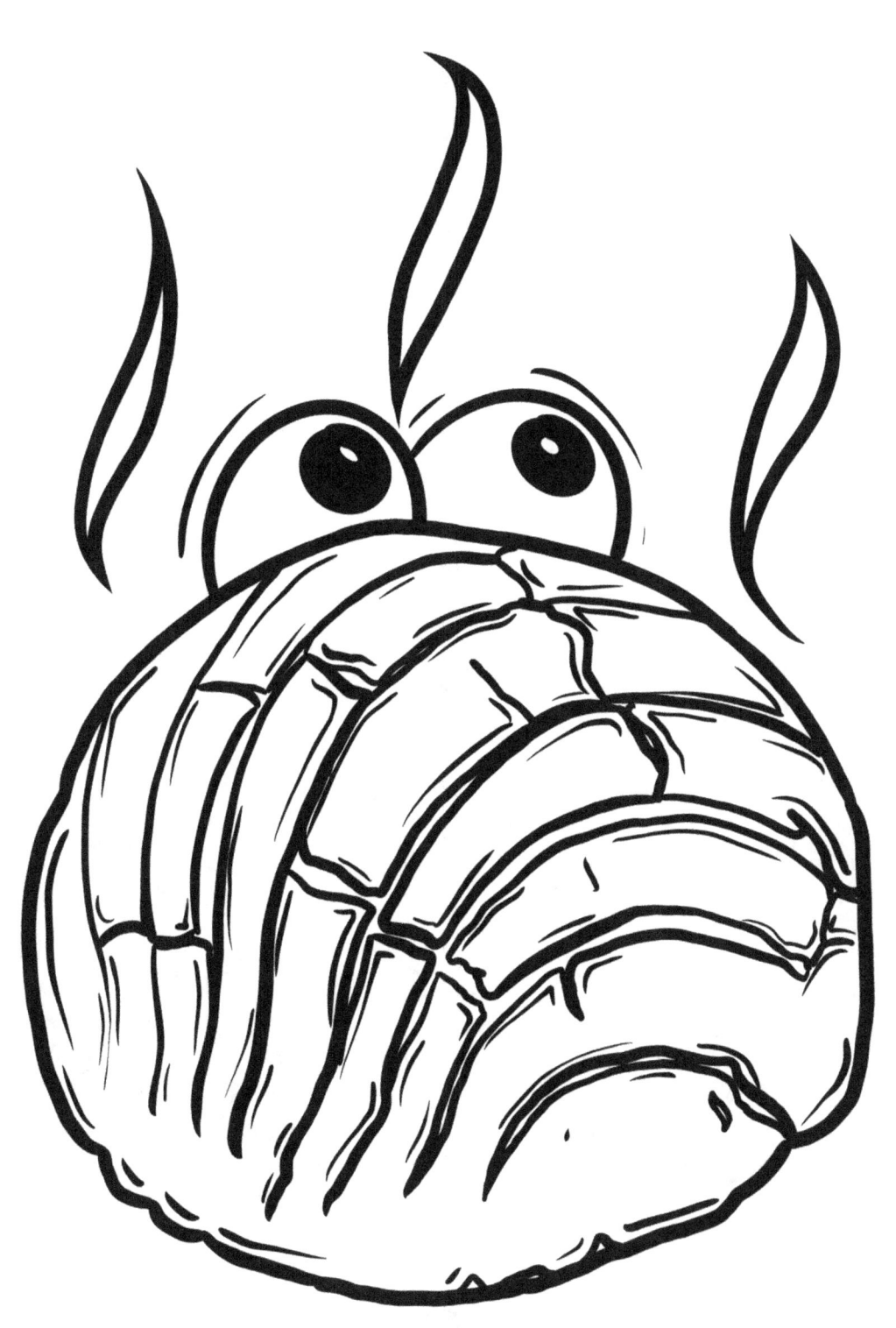

LA CONCHA

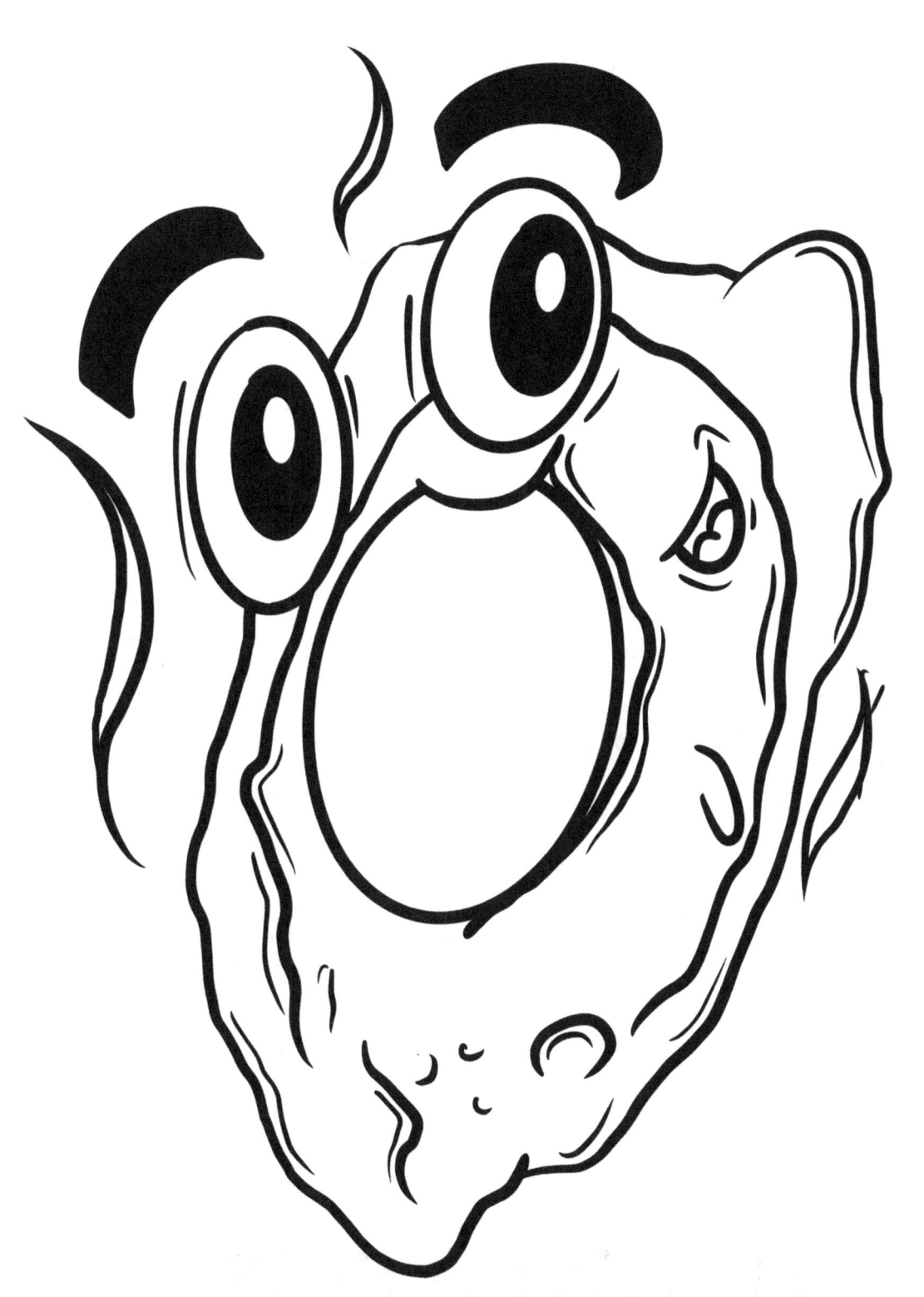

EL HUEVO FRITO

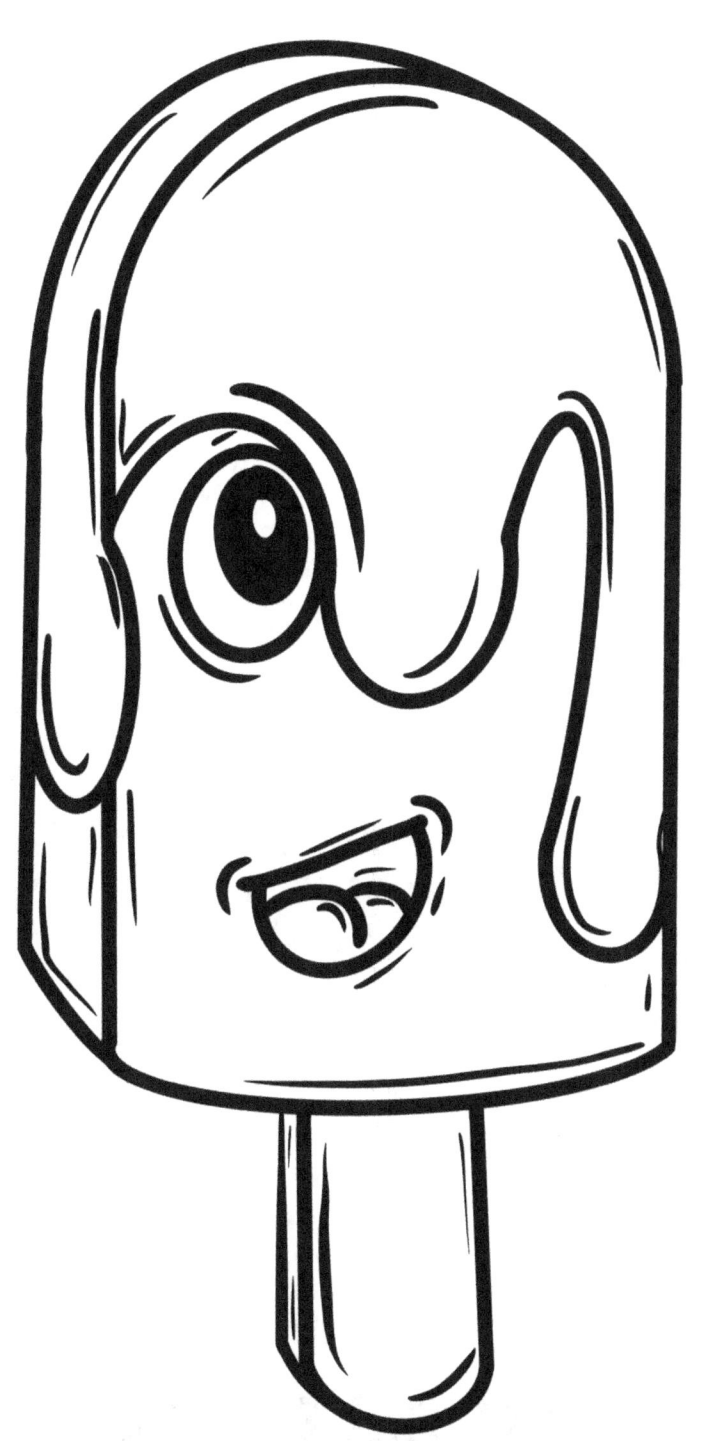

THE PALETA

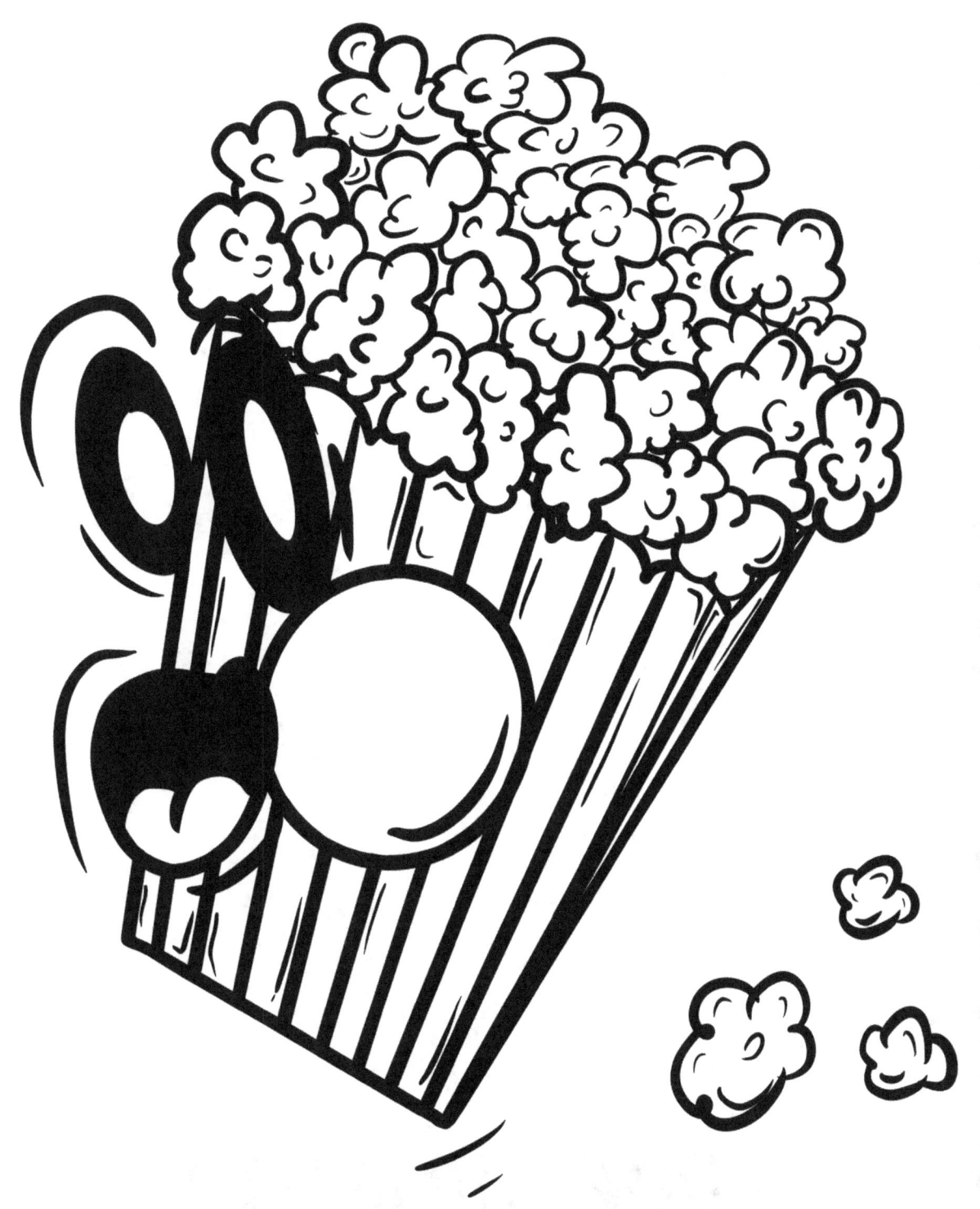

POPCORN KID

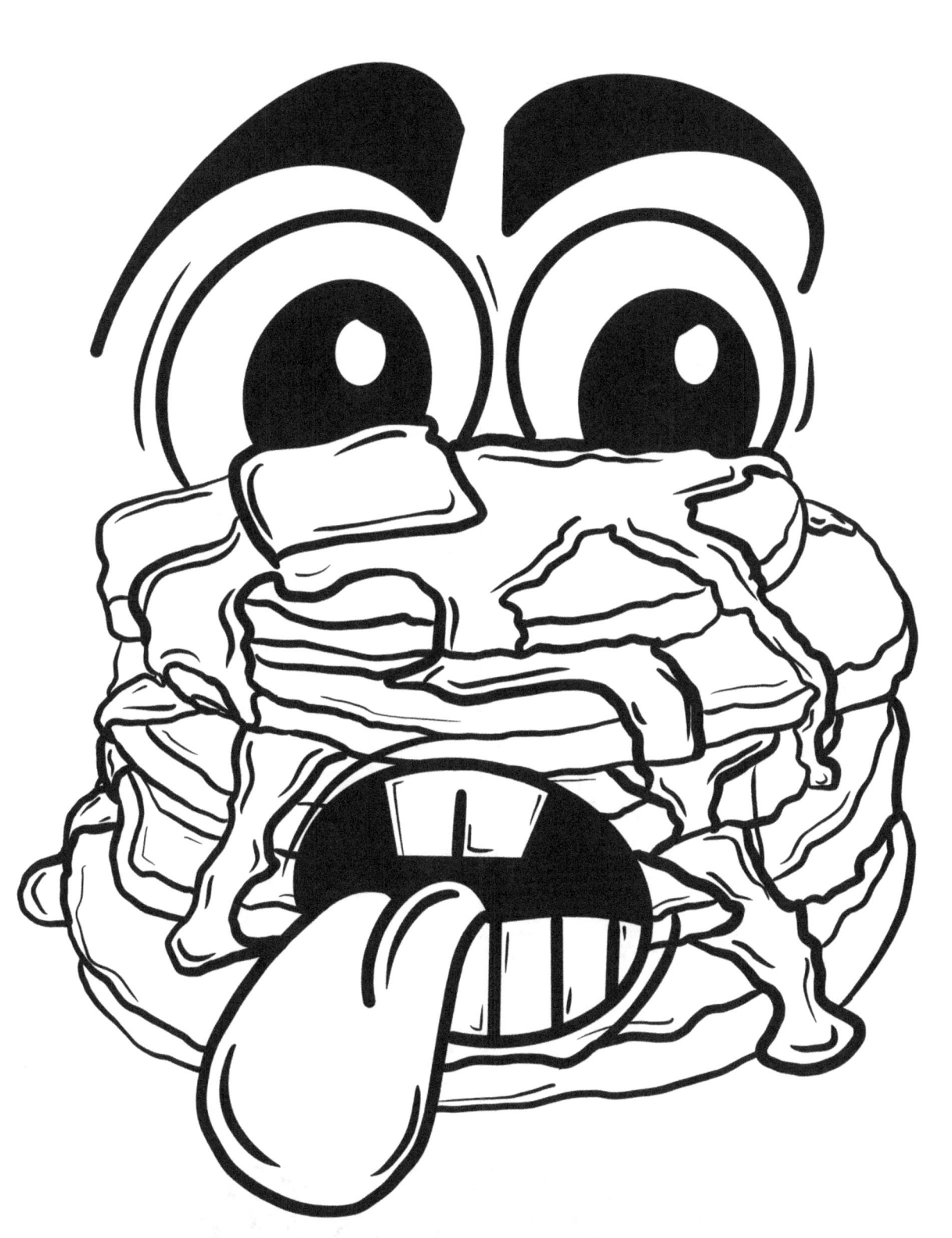

PANCAKE KING

www.ingramcontent.com/pod-product-compliance
Lightning Source LLC
Chambersburg PA
CBHW080443220526
45465CB00007B/2754